It's Praying Time!

&

OBEDIENCE IS REQUIRED!
Inspired By: God the Father
Written By: Dr. Kimberly K. Clayton

It's Praying Time & Obedience is Required!

Copyright © 2021 by Dr. Kimberly K Clayton

ISBN 978-0-578-97601-3

Self-Published Amazon KDP: Dr. Kimberly K. Clayton

itsprayingtime2020@gmail.com
Scriptures are noted from the following versions:

KJV – King James Version

NKJV – New King James Version

NLT – New Living Translation

AMP – Amplified

AMPC – Amplified Classic

TPT – The Passion Translation

TLB – The Living Bible

All rights reserved. No part of this book may be reproduced, stored in a retrieval system, or transmitted by any means or any form: electronic, mechanical, photocopy, recording, or any other, without permission in writing from the author.

Printed in the United States of America

Dr. Kimberly K. Clayton's Books:

1) It's Praying Time - What You Need to Know About Prayer Intercession

2) It's Praying Time & Soul Winning Time!

3) It's Praying Time & Humility is Required!

4) It's Praying Time & No More Idols!

Dedication

I dedicate this book to my late mother, Mrs. Millicent Jones who taught me at an early age that obedience to God is required. You made sure we understood that God was to be feared, respected and taken seriously.

Also to my daughter, Elise who even at a young age has shown a desire to obey God. Precious Elise, even at a young age you stand for God and his righteousness.

I also dedicate this book to my Grandmothers, Willene, Gracie and my bonus Grandmother (Great Aunt) Mary ☺. I have been extremely blessed to have praying Grandmothers like you, that pray and intercede for me and love me the way that you do!

Acknowledgments

I acknowledge God the Father, God the Son (Jesus Christ) and The Holy Spirit for their unconditional love and patience with me. I am forever grateful for all that God has done for me. Thank you for bringing the right people at the right time into my life. God I see you working in my life and I thank you for never giving up on me.

I am thankful for my earthly Dad, Mr. Jones who would encourage me not to give up and to keep going even when I was hard hit by circumstances in life.

To those of you who are apart of "It's Praying Time", I thank you for your faithfulness to pray with me, and for me and Elise. You too have become a part of our spiritual journey and I honor you for that.

Lastly to every faithful and humble Servant of God dedicated to do the work of the Lord, with obedience to God the Father. Please know your labor of love is not in vain, continue to obey God in spite of what others may think or say about you. I commend and celebrate your steadfast obedience to God, keep running for Jesus and don't give up now. May you be encouraged and strengthened for the journey ahead, and know that I applaud you and stand in the gap for you!

Table of Contents

Introduction	Pg. 11
Chapter 1: What is Obedience?	Pg. 14
Chapter 2: Who Should Obey God?	Pg. 22
Chapter 3: Why Does God Require Obedience?	Pg. 31
Chapter 4: How Is Obedience Shown to God?	Pg. 48
Chapter 5: When Is Obedience Shown to God?	Pg. 59
Chapter 6: Where Is Obedience Shown to God?	Pg. 67
Chapter 7: Summary & Salvation Prayer	Pg. 74
Author's Biography	Pg. 81

Introduction

Have you noticed how much disobedience takes place in the world today? There is no shortage of people disobeying God and the order that God is set forth for our lives. Watch a television show, watch a movie, read certain books, watch/read the news, watch how people drive, how they interact with each other, and how they handle bad news for one to see that obeying God is a real struggle for people.

There use to be a time in society where the majority of people actually made a consistent effort to obey Father God. Unfortunately the times that we live in the opposite is now true, the majority of people do not make a consistent effort to obey Father God on a daily basis. It has become the norm to pick and choose what one wants to obey. If one does not agree with God, one simply disobeys.

Amazingly society is out of control, and there are reasons for that. One of those reasons is disobedience to God and his order/structure for things. It's humbling to admit that Father God knows what's best for all of us and when we obey him life is so much better. Doesn't it make sense to turn back to God before it is too late? How good it is to come back to God through a devout obedience to him.

Oh that we would really understand that in these last and evil days that It's Praying Time & OBEDIENCE IS REQUIRED. Why do we expect things to go well for us or society, when the new thought is, "Do whatever you want, whenever you want. Do what you wanna do!"? Free will was not intended for us to continually choose disobedience that leads to death (natural and symbolic).

We want to make the most of every opportunity to win souls for Jesus Christ. The truth is eternity is closer for some than others. We are not just living for this life, but we are surely living for the life to come. Let me encourage you do not delay in saying this Salvation Prayer. Please repeat this prayer from a sincere heart.

Dear Lord Jesus, I know that I am a sinner, and I ask you for your forgiveness. I believe you died for my sins and rose from the dead. I turn from my sins, and invite You to come into my heart and life. I ask for the Holy Spirit to dwell in me, to guide me, and to teach me all things. I choose to trust and follow You as the Son of God and LORD and Savior in Jesus name Amen and Amen.

If you repeated that prayer with a true sincerity you JUST GOT SAVED!!! We encourage you to read your Bible on a daily basis. You can download the Bible

App at https://www.youversion.com/the-bible-app/. It will bless you greatly to be able to take the Bible with you everywhere you go. It even allows you to download offline versions of the Bible so you can still read the Bible without Internet access. This Bible App even reads the Bible to you, has devotionals, Bible study plans, prayers and more. Please get a paper Parallel Study Bible that has King James Version(KJV) and New Living Translation(NLT), or another version of your choice that helps you to understand the scriptures.

We are praying with you because getting saved is just the first step. Reading the Bible every day is the second step and the third step is to pray and ask God the Father to lead you to a church home where you will be planted, rooted and established in the Word of God. A good church home that teaches and preaches the Bible without watering it down. Many churches are still working for the Lord even if the doors of the church building are not physically open yet.

Lastly if you repeated the Salvation Prayer and got saved please email us at itsprayingtime2020@gmail.com, we would like to pray for you and encourage you along your spiritual journey. You can also email us your prayer requests and we would be glad to stand in the gap for you.

Chapter 1
What Is Obedience?

What is obedience? What is disobedience? Dictionary.com defines obedience as a compliance with an order, request, or law or submission to another's authority. The obedience synonyms are listed as follows compliance, acquiescence, dutifulness, duty, respect, conformity, and submissiveness. Dictionary.com defines disobedience as a failure to obey rules or someone in authority. Some of the disobedience synonyms are insubordination, unruliness, waywardness, indiscipline, bad behavior, misbehavior, misconduct, troublemaking, rebellion, defiance, revolt, lack of cooperation, noncompliance and contrariness.

Whenever we study the Old Testament and New Testament we can see that obedience has been a problem for people. God gave Adam specific instructions in the Garden of Eden. God made it clear that they were not to eat from the tree of the knowledge of good and evil. Genesis 2:17 KJV *But of the tree of the knowledge of good and evil, thou shalt not eat of it: for in the day that thou eatest thereof thou shalt surely die.* Did you notice that

God gave them the warning of what would happen if they disobeyed?

Father God knows best! When God tells us something we should be listening wholeheartedly. If God, requires obedience and then did not give us the warning of what would happen then that would be entirely different. That's how the enemy operates he tells some truths and/or complete lies but does not tell you the full consequences of your disobedience. I am so grateful that God does not operate that way. God tells us the commandment, law or instructions; then warns us what will happen when we don't obey.

Do you remember hearing the stories of God being a Vengeful God and a God of Wrath, especially in the Old Testament? Have you ever studied the history that the Israelites had with God? If not, now is a good time to do so. Even when the children of Israel were delivered from slavery and Pharoah in Egypt, they still had a very hard time trusting and obeying God. God provided manna from Heaven and the instructions were clear that on the sixth day they should gather enough for two days (the sixth and the seventh days). God wanted them to rest on the seventh day which is known as the Sabbath. Unfortunately the Israelites did not listen and tried to collect more than they should and guess what the food went bad. Even when the warning was not direct, it is clear that God wanted to know if they would walk in his ways, laws, and commandments. Would they obey? With God we know if we don't obey there will be a consequence, unless he decides to be merciful for a time.

Father God is the creator of all. We are his children. Doesn't the parent have the right to require obedience from his or her children? If there is a natural order to life on authority here on earth that parents are in charge and that the children must obey the parents. How much more we must understand spiritually that God the Father is in charge and that we are his children (even as adults) and we must obey him.

Father God has the right to require obedience from us. Obedience as a simplified definition is doing what God asks you to do the first time or immediately. It's hard to say we trust and love Father God, and outright refuse to obey him. Obedience and God go together very well, disobedience and God do not mix!

Obedience to God comes with a great deal of benefits. It's a blessing to know that children in a home with parents who had structure, raised the children to know that when they did their chores they got an allowance, extra time to stay up, movie nights, etc. However, if they did not do their chores they would be punished, no chores, go to bed earlier, no movie nights, etc.

Obedience is trusting and loving God enough to do what he tells us to do. Overall, have you ever observed how a small child usually just trusts his or her parents without question? That's how we should be with Father God, that we trust him without questioning, doubting and resisting the instructions he has given us. A small child is totally dependent on his or her parents, that's why it is critical that parents are submitted to God. When parents are obeying God, then children should be obeying parents, because one day those children will be older and need to know how to obey God consistently.

Obedience is consistently doing what God requires of us, even when we don't understand. It's hard to have a quality relationship with Father God if the basic foundation of obedience is constantly and blatantly ignored. Father God, is a good and loving God who desires to bless us and even when we disobey him he continues to bless us. Father God does not desire to punish us, but he can't allow persistent, consistent disobedience.

Just look at society today, it is clear that humanity is not obeying God. When obedience to God is there it is evident in the blessings from God. However, the opposite is true; when disobedience to God is there, it is evident in the punishments, chaos, confusion and destruction.

Obedience is respecting that God is the ultimate authority over our lives. God knows that if we are not submitted to him then it's going to be an even harder life than it should be. If God is the ultimate authority over one's life, then no room is left for the enemy to be the authority. God wants to protect us, but it is hard to be protected when we are not obeying his law, commands and instructions.

Obedience is choosing to live and serve God. If ever there were a time to choose this day who you will serve, it is indeed that time now. The choice should consistently be to live and serve God the remaining days of our lives. Believers have to set an example to this lost and dying world and a loving duty to obey God. A person really can't say they live for and serve God, but will not obey him.

Jesus was the epitome of OBEDIENCE! Jesus always did what the Father said to do. I really admired how Jesus consistently told the Jews, his disciples, and the enemy that he did not come to do his own will, but the will of his Father who sent him.

John 6:38-40 KJV **_For I came down from heaven, not to do mine own will, but the will of him that sent me._** _And this is the Father's will which hath sent me, that of all which he hath given me I should lose nothing, but should raise it up again at the last day. And this is the will of him that sent me, that every one which seeth the Son, and believeth on him, may have everlasting life: and I will raise him up at the last day._

John 6:38-40 NLT **_For I have come down from heaven to do the will of God who sent me, not to do my own will._** _And this is the will of God, that I should not lose even one of all those he has given me, but that I should raise them up at the last day. For it is my Father's will that all who see his Son and believe in him should have eternal life. I will raise them up at the last day."_

Heavenly Father thank you for helping me to understand what obedience to you means. Father God would you help me to learn what I need to know about obedience, so I can obey you even more. Lord God you are the way, the truth and the life no one can come to the Father except through Jesus Christ. Please Lord help me to obey you the first time and immediately without any hesitation. Father God would you help me to desire to live and serve you obediently the remaining days of my life?

Lord would you help me to understand that obedience is better than sacrifice? Lord God I desire to walk by faith through obedience to you, your laws, commandments and instructions in Jesus Mighty Name Amen and Amen.

Chapter 1 Summary

What Is Obedience?

- Obedience is doing what God says on a consistent basis immediately, the first time.

- Obedience is trusting and loving God to do what he says even when we don't understand.

- Submitting and respecting God's authority over our lives.

- Obedience is serving and living for Father God on a daily basis.

Chapter 2
Who Should Obey God?

Who should obey God? Everyone should obey God. It's interesting that when one is a child that obedience usually is taught and enforced. Yet, when one becomes an adult that it is assumed he or she is grown and can do whatever they want to do. I remember growing up with people who couldn't wait to be "GROWN" and now that they are, it's not what they thought it would be. Somewhere suffering has taken place for a lack of good teaching and because there is a great deal of disobedience. When one becomes an adult, he or she still needs to obey God.

Let's use this example. When a man asks a woman to marry him they are engaged. It's interesting that some men would like their soon to be wife to dress more modestly at this stage. One could think he is being controlling, but the other part is this there is more at stake now. He didn't work hard to save for a ring, for another man to come and steal his fiancé's heart away. If only we could see things from God's perspective, how much better it would be for us.

When we are children it is important to learn that you obey God, your parents, those that are in authority when they are not asking you to do something that is wrong. The basics of obedience should be taught at an early age and it should be explained in a way that a child understands. A child should be taught that we should obey God because he created us, he knows what's best for us and as we get older the consequences of not obeying (disobedience) are far greater as we grow older and become an adult. It's the truth that sets us free to live our best lives.

So, one can think that when I get GROWN I will do whatever I want, whenever I want. However, there are consequences for one's actions, good or bad. As we mature in our faith and relationship with God we should desire to obey God even when things aren't going as planned.

Obedience = Life and Disobedience = Death

If we remember this simplified equation, it will help us to go a long way in life. When we obey God that is the true roadmap to a Godly faith filled life, but when we disobey God that is a roadmap to serious consequences and can even lead to death. Life can be hard enough even when you obey, one should not want an even harder life for continuous disobedience. The way of the transgressor is hard is a scripture that cannot be denied. Proverbs 13:15 KJV *Good understanding giveth favor: but the way of transgressors is hard.* God's word warns us about not obeying him.

Of course the five-fold ministry should consistently do their utmost to obey God on a daily basis. Godly leadership has a far greater chance of leading people away from God, when they disobey. Again as you grow in the faith and mature in the weightier matters of God, there are serious consequences for knowing the right thing to do, but outright refusing to do it. As you go higher in God more is expected of you, and the obedience factor is even more intensified. As much is given much is required applies to Godly leaders. Luke 12:48 TPT *Every servant who does not know his master's will and unwittingly does what is wrong will receive a less severe punishment. For those who have received a greater revelation from their master are required a greater obedience. And those who have been entrusted with great responsibility will be held more responsible to their master."*

Godly leader, God is counting on you to lead people to him, not from him. That is why it is critical to know as one of his Godly leaders you must obey him, through a consistent obedient lifestyle. People who are weak in the faith are watching you, people who are unbelievers are watching you too. It can be sad and unfortunate to know that some won't attend church anymore because of what they saw, heard and experienced. One can desire the titles in the church and Kingdom of God, however one must really know what it takes to carry the title. One of the requirements to carry the title is OBEDIENCE IS REQUIRED.

The furnace has been turned up, this is the time to do what God requires of us without excuses. God's leaders must be a shining example of Godly obedience to God, his word, laws, commandments and instructions. With the furnace being turned up and it's the last of the last and evil days entirely too much is at stake, especially for a lost and dying world that we live in.

The world's thought is as a leader is promoted that they do less work because they can delegate the work and have people cater to there every need. God's leadership model is really the opposite. Jesus did not come to be served, but to serve. Mark 10:45 KJV *For even the Son of Man came not to be ministered unto, but to minister and to give His life as a ransom for many.* The body of Christ has the Servant Leadership Model to follow and to embrace. So, we need to understand that as God promotes us we are held to a much higher standard, and that means a higher level of obedience to God. God's leaders must fully understand that as God calls them higher they cannot go down to a lower level of obedience, that they must go to a higher level of obedience to God the Father. The common thought of God understands me and knows my heart, can no longer stand in the way of the obedience that is required of us.

If even Jesus obeyed Father God, then why do we think we don't have too? Jesus was the ULTIMATE example of obedience. It is critical that we as believers follow his lead. Jesus consistently pointed out that he came to do the will of his Father, not his own will. Jesus fully understood that there is DIVINE ORDER in the Kingdom of God. That DIVINE ORDER starts with OBEDIENCE to God. Obedience is one of the KEYS to the Kingdom of God. It's hard to do great things for God without obedience.

Even Jesus had to obey the will of God concerning the crucifixion. Jesus's agony is on full display in the Garden of Gethsemane. Jesus prayed earnestly three times, but by the third time Jesus accepts the will of God. If Jesus had not obeyed God, there would be no hope or promise of eternal salvation. When one does not obey God, there are consequences not just for us but for the Kingdom of God too. The more we see the chaos, destruction and confusion it is clear that obedience is a low priority for so many. That has to change quickly in this hour, OBEDIENCE TO GOD and God's order has to be a TOP priority consistently from this moment forward.

We can no longer say to our children and those under our authority, DO AS I SAY, NOT AS I DO. The double standard is costing us entirely too much. People need to see us live an obedient life to God, a life that glorifies God. When we really live for God it shows, then when we say that obedience to God is key it carries far more weight because we ourselves are obedient to God. Is it quite possible that some people don't take us seriously because we are not consistent with our walk with God? The enemy can be crafty and tell us that now that we are adults we don't have to live the standard that is required of children. That simply is not true, actually as adults more is required of us especially in the area of obedience.

We should not want to bear the burden, sin and consequences of leading our families away from God. While there is still time let's vow to live obedient lifestyles before God, let's have a determination to let go of everything that is keeping us from obeying God. Remember the saying that misery loves company is so true. As you are determined to live more obediently to God, please know that you will have to separate yourself from some people (even places and things too).

As you let your light shine more and more, it will be hard for those who disobey God to be around you. It's not that you are pointing out their disobedience verbally, but your obedience shines bright and it provokes them. Be prepared for backlash, hostility, throwing your past in your face, and even false accusations as you continue to obey God. Everyone will not be happy that you are choosing to obey God, so be prepared that even family, friends and those you have helped the most to have a problem with your determination to obey Father God.

If we are not teaching our children to obey God, be rest assured the enemy and this world will teach them not to. That's why it is crucial that we teach our children the foundation of obedience while they are still young. When we grasp that our teaching is not only what we say verbally, but what we actually live before them then we are really setting the right and best example before them.

There will come a time no matter how blessed you are financially, physically, mentally, emotionally, and spiritually that you will need God to remember you and your family. Life gets really hard and tough at times, therefore it is vital that we live an obedient lifestyle that brings God the glory. No one gets through this life without heartaches, pain and suffering, but it's better to go through all of that with God than without him. The reality is that no can say they don't need God; so doesn't it make sense to obey him in good and bad times? God is the only one that can deliver us in serious times of trouble, so it should motivate us even more to live obediently for Father God.

We have to remember that we demonstrate our faith through obedience. It's hard to say that one is a person of faith, but refuse to obey God. Obedience and faith go hand in hand.

Chapter 2 – Summary

Who Should Obey God?

- **EVERYONE**

- **Especially the five-fold ministry: Apostles, Prophets, Evangelists, Pastors, Teachers**

- **The world is watching, we must be the example that God has always called for.**

- **Our children and youth are watching, we have to show them an obedient lifestyle to God.**

- **Our faith is demonstrated through obedience.**

Chapter 3
Why Does God Require Obedience?

Why does God require obedience? Let's go back to the saying Father God knows best. The God of all creation knows what's best for humanity. Since he knows what's best for us doesn't it make sense to obey his commands, instructions and laws that govern our lives. God did not make laws and commands to merely control us like puppets. Father God's law, commands and instructions are there to protect us from harming others and ourselves.

Let's just look at society today under the saying, "You can do whatever you want, whenever you want." The news headlines will tell you easily that saying is not working for society today. The amount of destruction, chaos and confusion that we see in the world today is because so many people have been deceived in to believing that they truly can do whatever they want, whenever they want. Humanity's decisions and choices have good or bad consequences. If one deliberately chooses to drive at high speed down the street, most likely they will crash into an innocent bystander. The temptation is to drive fast, but the reality is someone will be injured or killed for this reckless act.

Not obeying God is not working for society. Crime is up in just about every category! Overall most people have admitted that they don't trust most people, they don't feel safe and some no longer watch the news because of the stories. Even in life and death situations it is hard to get some people to cooperate with simple instructions. Again these are all indications people refuse to obey God but believe that life will go well for them, even when they are not making wise choices.

Sometimes it would be wise just to stop and think about decisions before they were made. A good question to ask oneself is this, "What are the consequences of not obeying?" See at the time it may not seem like such a big deal that one isn't doing what God told him or her to do. Yet the harsh reality is disobedience brings sin which can lead to death. Even when it is not the actual death of one's life, it can be the symbolic death of a marriage ending in divorce, a career shattered by scandal, a friendship ruined by betrayal, family relationships hurt by drug addiction, a loved one incarcerated for life, an injury that causes permanent paralysis, are just a few examples of symbolic death that stemmed from disobedience to God.

Even in Biblical times when someone disobeyed God the consequence of that sin was usually in a way that could not be ignored. King David had a heart after God, yet his flesh was flawed just like any other human. It was also clear that King David would run back to God when he disobeyed and sinned against God. Yet, King David was not spared the consequences of his sin, the punishment was usually intense. King David committed adultery, murder and tried to cover it up. He broke several of God's commandments, Thou shall not commit adultery, Thou shall not kill, and Thou shall not covet. Unfortunately King David and Bathsheba's first born child, does not survive. As the Prophet Nathan makes it clear that "the sword" would not depart from King David's house. Read 2 Samuel 12:1-23 KJV for more understanding.

As you read and study more about King David you will see, it is true that "the sword" (trouble, calamity, tragedy) was on his house, King David had to run from many enemies including one of his son's! It was clear that King David was held to a higher standard. People following the leader can be deceived into thinking that they too can, disobey God and that's not true. This should serve as a reminder to the body of the Christ, especially to those who serve as an Apostle, Prophet, Prophetess, Evangelist, Pastor and Teacher.

Let's explore in the Bible what happened when individuals thought they did not have to obey God. Let's start with the Prophet Jonah.

Jonah 1:1-4 NKJV *Now the word of the LORD came to Jonah the son of Amittai, saying, "Arise, go to Nineveh, that great city, and cry out against it; for their wickedness has come up before Me." But Jonah arose to flee to Tarshish from the presence of the LORD. He went down to Joppa, and found a ship going to Tarshish; so he paid the fare, and went down into it, to go with them to Tarshish from the presence of the LORD. But the LORD sent out a great wind on the sea, and there was a mighty tempest on the sea, so that the ship was about to be broken up.*

Notice that Jonah was told specific instructions by God, but Jonah decided he would not obey and actually went the opposite direction. Jonah seems to think he can escape the assignment that God has given him. Not so! Even while on the ship suddenly a raging storm comes out of nowhere to the point, it would have torn the ship apart. Please note the storm coming out of nowhere is no coincidence, God is definitely trying to get Jonah's attention.

Jonah 1:5-11 NKJV *Then the mariners were afraid; and every man cried out to his god, and threw the cargo that was in the ship into the sea, to lighten the load. But Jonah had gone down into the lowest parts of the ship, had lain down, and was fast asleep. So the captain came to him, and said to him, "What do you mean, sleeper? Arise, call on your God; perhaps your God will consider us, so that we may not perish." And they said to one another, "Come, let us cast lots, that we may know for whose cause this trouble has come upon us." So they cast lots, and the lot fell on Jonah. Then they said to him, "Please tell us! For whose cause is this trouble upon us? What is your occupation? And where do you come from? What is your country? And of what people are you?" So he said to them, "I am a Hebrew; and I fear the LORD, the God of heaven, who made the sea and the dry land. Then the men were exceedingly afraid, and said to him, "Why have you done this?" For the men knew that he fled from the presence of the LORD, because he had told them. Then they said to him, "What shall we do to you that the sea may be calm for us?"—for the sea was growing more tempestuous.*

So, as it would be Jonah is fast asleep while this raging storm is getting worse. The men on the ship have to wake him up, they ask questions and cast lots to see who has brought this trouble and it points to Jonah. Isn't interesting that these men had done nothing to provoke the wrath of God but Jonah's disobedience did. They even cry out why has Jonah fled the presence of God, in other words why didn't you obey God? Do you see what is happening to us, because of your disobedience? Yet, the men have the wisdom to know that Jonah has the answer to calming this storm.

Jonah 1:12-17 NKJV *And he said to them, "Pick me up and throw me into the sea; then the sea will become calm for you. For I know that this great tempest is because of me. "Nevertheless the men rowed hard to return to land, but they could not, for the sea continued to grow more tempestuous against them. Therefore they cried out to the L*ORD *and said, "We pray, O L*ORD*, please do not let us perish for this man's life, and do not charge us with innocent blood; for You, O L*ORD*, have done as it pleased You." So they picked up Jonah and threw him into the sea, and the sea ceased from its raging. Then the men feared the LORD exceedingly, and offered a sacrifice to the L*ORD *and took vows. Now the L*ORD *had prepared a great fish to swallow Jonah. And Jonah was in the belly of the fish three days and three nights.*

I found it interesting that even when the men were told to throw Jonah overboard they did not want to do that. They tried to row the boat harder towards land. When they saw that would not work they were moved to pray that Jonah's life would not be charged to them, because they realized it was God causing the storm and then threw Jonah overboard, then they even offered a sacrifice to the LORD and took vows. It seems that these unbelievers may have converted to believers, even in Jonah's disobedience it still worked for the good.

Unfortunately for Jonah he is placed on a divine time out when he is swallowed by the fish and in its belly for three days. Now Jonah knows, what??? He can't outrun God. When God says you have to do something, please just obey the consequences are too great when we disobey God Almighty.

Now read Jonah 2:1-10 NKJV, this is where Jonah has to cry out to God.

Then Jonah prayed to the LORD his God from the fish's belly. And he said: "I cried out to the LORD because of my affliction, And He answered me. "Out of the belly of Sheol I cried, And You heard my voice. For You cast me into the deep, Into the heart of the seas, And the floods surrounded me; All Your billows and Your waves passed over me. Then I said, 'I have been cast out of Your sight; Yet I will look again toward Your holy temple.' The waters surrounded me, even to my soul; The deep closed around me; Weeds were wrapped around my head. I went down to the moorings of the mountains; The earth with its bars closed behind me forever; Yet You have brought up my life from the pit, O LORD, my God. "When my soul fainted within me, I remembered the LORD; And my prayer went up to You, Into Your holy temple. "Those who regard worthless idols Forsake their own Mercy. But I will sacrifice to You With the voice of thanksgiving; I will pay what I have vowed. Salvation is of the LORD." So the LORD spoke to the fish, and it vomited Jonah onto dry land.

When Jonah cried out in sincerity to the LORD and said he would pay what he vowed, God could release him from the fish. In this prayer one can see that Jonah is genuinely sorry and shows the LORD a heart of repentance. If Jonah, would not have been serious about his disobedience it's a strong possibility he would have ended up in the belly of the fish a lot longer than three days.

Let's read Jonah 3:1-4 NKJV *Now the word of the LORD came to Jonah the second time, saying, "Arise, go to Nineveh, that great city, and preach to it the message that I tell you." So Jonah arose and went to Nineveh, according to the word of the LORD. Now Nineveh was an exceedingly great city, a three-day journey in extent. And Jonah began to enter the city on the first day's walk. Then he cried out and said, "Yet forty days, and Nineveh shall be overthrown!"*

God, is so good! He gives Jonah another chance to do what he told him to do. Jonah has learned his lesson and does what the LORD has instructed him to do, this time without hesitation. The LORD knows that some things may seem too scary to us, but we still have to obey him. God will redeem us, he wants us to carry out his plans for this earth we have to be willing and obedient.

As we read further into Chapter three of Jonah we find out what happens. Jonah 3:5-9 NKJV *So the people of Nineveh believed God, proclaimed a fast, and put on sackcloth, from the greatest to the least of them. Then word came to the king of Nineveh; and he arose from his throne and laid aside his robe, covered himself with sackcloth and sat in ashes. And he caused it to be proclaimed and published throughout Nineveh by the decree of the king and his nobles, saying, Let neither man nor beast, herd nor flock, taste anything; do not let them eat, or drink water. But let man and beast be covered with sackcloth, and cry mightily to God; yes, let every one turn from his evil way and from the violence that is in* his hands. Who can tell if God will turn and relent, and turn away from His fierce anger, so that we may not perish?

Isn't this amazing, the people Nineveh humbled themselves! The King first humbles himself by covering himself with sackcloth and ashes. Let's look at what putting sackcloth and sitting in ashes means. **According to Gotquestions.org (April 26, 2021) in Biblical Times the sackcloth was an uncomfortable clothing that was most likely made of goat hair. When one would wear sackcloth and sit in ashes it meant a sign of repentance for the wrong one had done and/or the pronouncement of destruction to come. It showed God the inner reflection of true humility taken place in one's heart.**

Then the King proclaims a Kingdom wide fast. The fast that the King decreed was a serious fast too, no food or water for the people and animals too. Everyone had to fast! The King knew the evil ways and violence of the people and Kingdom would no longer be tolerated, so the people were told to let their wicked ways go! They have hope that if they fast and let go of their wickedness God will have mercy on them, and not destroy the city of Nineveh.

What happens? Let's keep reading to find out. Jonah 3:10 NKJV *Then God saw their works, that they turned from their evil way; and God relented from the disaster that He had said He would bring upon them, and He did not do it.* Wow, it's a miracle the city of Nineveh was not destroyed, even though they deserved it. Nineveh's heartfelt, repentance and humility was sufficient to spare them the destruction that they had brought on themselves through wickedness and violence.

Has trouble come to your family, in a way that it cannot be ignored? I mean persistent trouble, perhaps the kind that makes the news, even CNN news; worldwide news?? It may be quite possible that someone or several relatives within a family are not obeying the call of God on their life. When Jonah obeyed the second time, look at the difference it made for the city of Nineveh. More times than not people are looking for a solid spiritual leader that they can see, talk to and look up to. You may be the one that helps to keep your family from going astray, especially in these last of the last and evil days. God wants to use you for his glory, answer the call today and obey God with your whole heart, mind and soul.

If you know in your heart, that you are refusing to answer the call of God on your life; please note this is the time to give God a sincere and repentant yes because time is running out. Do your best not to come grudgingly to the LORD, after all he has been very patient with you. Sometimes we really don't understand all that is at stake when we refuse to obey God. It can even be for a lack of good teaching too, that still does not give us license to persist at disobedience.

The scriptures make it clear that our children unfortunately suffer for our disobedience. As you study King David's life once the sword is upon his house, his son tries to kill him, but ends up dying tragically and one of his daughter's suffers through a tragic ordeal. Numbers 14:18 AMP *'The LORD is slow to anger, and abundant in lovingkindness, forgiving wickedness and transgression; but He will by no means clear the guilty, visiting (avenging) the wickedness and guilt of the fathers on the children, to the third and fourth generations [that is, calling the children to account for the sins of their fathers].'* As we read this scripture and others that are very similar it is clear that parents need to obey God. When they don't most likely their children will also suffer for the parents disobedience.

As we look at society, one has to really think it through what's happening right now. Some children have not lived long enough to suffer some of the consequences that have happened to them. Hosea

4:6 AMPC *My people are destroyed for lack of knowledge; because you [the priestly nation] have rejected knowledge, I will also reject you that you shall be no priest to Me; seeing you have forgotten the law of your God, I will also forget your children.* Hosea 4:6 is ringing louder and louder. As Believers we cannot afford to live like the world does, we have to obey God the consequences are far too great and impact our children too.

If there were ever a time that we needed God to remember our children it is now. Our children have been under attack by the enemy for quite some time. Usually when something terrible happens it is the usual custom for one to show God humility. There are some events that cause us to pause and ask God why has this happened? Or why does this keep happening to our children, family, friends, neighbors, community, etc.?

Another view point is this, some of our spiritual giants and generals have done all that they could do, and served the LORD faithfully and honorably. 2 Timothy 4:7-8 KJV *I have fought a good fight, I have finished my course, I have kept the faith: Henceforth there is laid up for me a crown of righteousness, which the Lord, the righteous judge, shall give me at that day: and not to me only, but unto all them also that love his appearing.* Shouldn't we be in position when it's time for them to pass the baton??? Especially when we can see how short time is, God needs our yes now and our OBEDIENCE IS REQUIRED consistently. So, we can't do anything about time that has been wasted, but we can start with right now this very moment to obey God concerning the callings on our lives and his specific instructions too.

It can be a sad situation to take our spiritual giants and generals for granted. Especially when they have lived a very long time, we should realize at some point they will be called home to be with the LORD. Let's cherish and appreciate the spiritual giants and generals that we have left and learn all that we can from them, especially while they are still in the land of the living. You may never know what God really has in mind for you and your future, so obey him and serve him wholeheartedly while you can. There may be a reason you have to work with a certain leader, learn all that you can because one day they won't be here anymore.

If you can avoid the "double grief" I encourage you to do so. "Double grief" is the natural grief of losing your mentor and the spiritual grief of knowing that you did not listen to God or your mentor's instructions; and did not bother to learn all that you could from them while you had the time. God can and will heal you of the "double grief" if that's the place you find yourself now. The best lesson is to learn from those mistakes of disobedience and begin to live a life of obedience that pleases and glorifies Father God. **We shouldn't let the past beat us down, but we should definitely learn from it so we can do better the next time around.**

Why else, should we obey God? Like the Saints of Old would say, "There is no need for God to give you the next assignment, when you haven't finished the last assignment." It's important to obey God and finish each assignment. Unfortunately some have asked God for different or new assignments, but have failed to finish the current assignment(s) they are on. In these last of the last and evil days it is important to finish the assignments that God gives us to do. Each assignment is really preparing us for the next level, for the next assignment. If one can't be trusted to finish at this level, one can't expect that God would promote them to the next level and assignment. So, it's simple obey God and his instructions and finish, then you can get the next assignment.

Heavenly Father, would you help me to fully understand the consequences of my disobedience? As I learn those consequences may I use them as reminders to consistently obey you, especially in these last of the last and evil days. God only you know what you have in store for me, I need your guidance and instructions to make wise decisions. Lord when I am tempted not to obey, please send loving reminders to stay on the course that you have for me. Lord as I have learned that it will impact my children, my family, myself and society too help me to know that I can make a difference with my obedience to you. Father God as I learn that the spiritual baton has to be passed, please prepare me in advance to be ready to accept the spiritual baton when it is passed. Help me to obey the call of my life and walk obediently by faith and not by sight in Jesus Mighty Name Amen and Amen.

Chapter 3 Summary

Why Does God Require Obedience?

- There are serious consequences for disobedience to God.

- Society becomes a place of confusion, chaos and destruction.

- Our children, families and societies suffer for our disobedience.

- God wants to spare us, but we have to obey him.

- We need to be prepared when the spiritual baton is passed to us.

- It is possible to avoid "double grief".

- If you find yourself in "double grief" now is the time to learn from it.

- We need God to remember our children.

- So God can give you, the next assignment.

Chapter 4

How Is Obedience Shown to God?

How is obedience shown to God? By doing what he has told us to do in the Bible and what he has told us to do specifically. Remember the acronym for Bible:

B-Basic
I-Instruction
B-Before
L-Leaving
E-Earth

Father God knows what's best and has been so kind to leave us the Bible that does give us instructions on how to navigate this life we live, to avoid some of the hard knocks and bruises, temptations, and traps that the enemy has set for us. Yet, if we aren't reading the Bible on a daily basis it is hard to know some of the basic instructions that God has already left for us. Daily Bible reading is a necessity to learn what God has told us and what he requires of us.

We won't be able to say that we didn't know this or that. There is no shortage of the Bible and Biblical material that prevents us from learning all that we can learn about God and his instructions. The day of just being Bible illiterate has to come to an end asap.

The Body of the Christ needs the five fold ministry (Apostle, Prophet, Prophetess, Evangelist, Pastor & Teacher) each serves a critical role and function to help develop, grow and mature the church. The majority of Pastors have emphasized for a quite sometime that we need to stay in the Word (keep reading, studying, meditating, memorizing and praying the Bible) on a daily basis.

It's God's word that will make the ultimate difference in our lives. Yet if we are not opening the Bible and reading it each day we are missing one of the most important encounters that we could have with God. Before our day gets busy, the first thing we should do is get up and read the Bible and pray to God, and listen for his instructions for the day. If you haven't ever done that, oh what a difference you will see in each day. It's a real blessing to live intentionally and purposefully for Father God, but it's hard to accomplish without starting the day reading the Bible and praying.

How else do we obey God? Through a solid prayer life! If obedience to God has been a real struggle in one's life, it is important that one spends even more time in prayer to God about that. God desires to work with us and even partner with us on this journey but we have to be willing to admit that we need his help. Prayer is key in this area. Sometimes we might not even be aware that we struggle with obedience. That is why it is important that one ask God:

What areas need improvement in my life?

Father God do I struggle with obedience?

Father God could you show me where I have not obeyed you?

Father God what scriptures on obedience should I study today?

Father God the last time you told me to do something did I do it?

Did I complete the task the way you instructed me to? It's important to learn to wait for the answer from God. As God answers these questions it is important to be honest with one's self, and make the necessary adjustments and changes to be more obedient to God. As God reveals things to you and about you, it can be a surprise to see that you aren't where you thought you actually were in the obedience area. Sometimes we can obey God in part, we are striving to obey Father God in whole, in every area of our lives.

Also as you pray, it is wisdom to pray God's words back to him, especially in the area of obedience. Remember we pray God's word back to him because his word cannot come back void to him. Praying the obedience scriptures over one's life is key to a major breakthrough to increasing obedience to Father God. Obedience to God is a critical area and should not be taken or handled lightly. Remember obedience is one of the keys to living a successful faith filled life. It should not be any wonder that the enemy works so hard to tempt people not to obey God and his Holy instructions too. Prayer is a surefire way to help protect one from the pitfalls and traps of this life.

It is good to read the Bible, but to go higher is to study, meditate and memorize key scriptures on obedience. That is why it is very important to have a paper study Bible as well. The online and digital Bible's are great but it is important to have a Bible that doesn't require Internet access, batteries or electricity. As God speaks to you while you study his Holy word, write notes and dates in the Bible. As you walk on this faith journey you will need loving reminders and encouragement to keep going on this journey. It's nothing like opening the Bible to find that on this day, month, year and time God spoke to your heart about this particular scripture and what he revealed to you.

As one meditates (thinks about consistently) and memorizes scriptures on obedience, it is important to put those scriptures deep in our hearts. Even King David knew that is how he would not sin against God, by hiding God's word deep in his heart. Psalm 119:10-11 KJV *With my whole heart have I sought Thee; O let me not wander from Thy commandments! Thy word have I hid in mine heart, that I might not sin against Thee.*

The more one meditates and memorizes the obedience scriptures, the more one's heart fills up on those obedience scriptures. Remember God knows us through and through, people look on the outer appearance of a person but Father God looks at the heart of the person. Jeremiah 17:10 KJV *"I, the LORD, search the heart; I try the reins, even to give every man according to his ways, and according to the fruit of his doings."* What a blessing it would be for God to find that our hearts are filled with his obedience scriptures.

It's also good to have a notebook or a prayer journal that you take notes in and write reflections as you study, meditate and memorize God's Holy words. Why do we write things down? So, we can remember them. That's a very important part of studying the Bible, writing notes and what God reveals to you will help you to remember what God is saying to you. Also, the times that we live in have a way of bringing a great deal of stress into our everyday lives, so we need tools that helps us to remember what God has said so we can continue do what he asks of us.

Personally in my own life, it has been such a blessing to have journals of different sizes. The small journal was a gift for obtaining my Minister's License. It has been such a blessing to write down God given dreams, goals, instructions and visions for my life in this small journal. As I write the books that God is calling me to write, it has blessed me immensely to go back to the list and check off what has been accomplished for God's glory. Again though, I could not achieve God's vision for my life if I continued to walk in disobedience. I had to learn to be consistent and faithful in the area of obedience to reap the full benefits and blessings from God. I like the way the Saints of Old would say, "There's no need in asking God for the next assignment, when the last assignment was not completed."

OBEDIENCE IS REQUIRED, is not just the title of this book but a message from God that the Body of Christ has to obey him whole heartedly. It will be harder and harder to live in this world without obeying God. We are living in times where we really need to know God and obey him. See it's one thing to know of God and a whole another thing to know him more intimately and personally. The same can be said for it's one thing to know God, but it is even better to obey him.

Another way we obey God is raising our children for him. God's word instructs us to raise our children and the future generations according to his words, laws, commandments and instructions. One of the ways we raise our children for God is through our loving and obedient example. The children need to see adults that love and obey God. If ever there was a time to be better Godly role models for the children now is that time. Especially when we can see that our children as a whole are under attack by the enemy. We have to take a stronger stand for the children, and one of the ways that we do that is to raise our children for Father God.

Proverbs 22:6 KJV *Train up a child in the way he should go, and when he is old he will not depart from it.*

Isaiah 54:13 KJV *And all thy children shall be taught of the Lord, and great shall be the peace of thy children.*

Psalm 78:4-8 KJV *We will not hide them from their children, showing to the generation to come the praises of the Lord and His strength, and His wonderful works that He hath done. For He established a testimony in Jacob and appointed a law in Israel, which He commanded to our fathers, that they should make them known to their children; that the generation to come might know them, even the children who should be born, who should arise and declare them to their children, that they might set their hope in God and not forget the works of God, but keep His commandments; and so might not be as their fathers, a stubborn and rebellious generation, a generation that set not their heart aright, and whose spirit was not steadfast with God.*

Deuteronomy 11:18-21 KJV *"Therefore shall ye lay up these my words in your heart and in your soul, and bind them for a sign upon your hand, that they may be as frontlets between your eyes. And ye shall teach them to your children, speaking of them when thou sittest in thine house and when thou walkest by the way, when thou liest down and when thou risest up. And thou shalt write them upon the doorposts of thine house and upon thy gates, that your days may be multiplied, and the days of your children, in the land which the LORD swore unto your fathers to give them, as the days of heaven upon the earth.*

We have to remember that if we don't raise our children to follow God in his ways, precepts, laws, commandments and instructions, unfortunately the world will teach them not to follow God and his Holy words. I have met many parents who have major regrets of not raising their children to live for Father God by following Jesus Christ's example and teachings. Now they realize that's the solid rock foundation that their children are missing. Unfortunately it is more of struggle to get them to attend church services, Sunday school, Bible class, prayer meetings/services, etc. all because when the children were young they were not raised for God's glory.

Unfortunately many have been deceived into believing that a child should have a choice on being raised for God. We have to remember that Father God is a God of order, structure and stability. God has an order that parents are in charge, and children need to know that early on. As adults we have the power to help set some things back in order, but we must do it God's way. Even when the world tries to teach our children contrary to God's word, when we have trained them in Godly instructions and raised them for God's glory they will not be deceived by what the world has to offer.

God is calling us to raise our children for him in a way that does not bring confusion to them. One of the ways we avoid this confusion is by living a way that does not contradict God's words before them, yet tell them they have to obey the good we teach. How many of us know the truth here? It really does not work that way. That's the world's way, "Do as I say, Not as I do." God's way, "Do as I say, Do as I do." God's ways and standards are higher and better than our ways. God created us and he knows what is best for us.

Isaiah 55:8-9 KJV *For my thoughts are not your thoughts, neither are your ways my ways, saith the Lord. For as the heavens are higher than the earth, so are my ways higher than your ways, and my thoughts than your thoughts.*

Heavenly Father thank you for giving me strategies and insights to help me obey you and your Holy word, instructions, laws and commandments. Father God I want to live a life that glorifies you and shows my love, devotion and obedience to you. Father God do I struggle to obey your laws and commandments? Father God would you help me to read, study, meditate, memorize and pray your scriptures on obedience? I desire to bury you word in my heart so I will not sin against you, Father God. Lord God please help me to raise my children for you. Lord God please instruct me in your ways so I can live an obedient lifestyle before you and others. May my lifestyle of obedience win many souls for you in Jesus Mighty Name Amen and Amen.

Chapter 4 Summary

How is Obedience Shown to God?

- **By obeying what God has told us to do.**

- **By reading God's Bible every day.**

- **By studying, meditating, memorizing and praying God's words.**

- **By hiding God's word's deep in our hearts.**

- **By raising our children for God.**

- **By living a God obedient lifestyle before God and others.**

- **Understanding God's way, "Do as I say, Do as I do."**

Chapter 5
When Is Obedience Shown to God?

When is obedience shown to God? Obedience is shown to God immediately. It has been said that delayed obedience is DISOBEDIENCE. When you look at it that way, you understand that is better to obey God right away. It may not seem like it at the time but delayed disobedience are actually signs of mistrust and fear.

We have to get to a point that we are just like Mary and say, "be it unto me according to thy word."

Luke 1:38 KJV *And Mary said, Behold the handmaid of the Lord; be it unto me according to thy word. And the angel departed from her.*

Luke 1:38 TPT *Then Mary responded, saying, "Yes! I will be a mother for the Lord! As his servant, I accept whatever he has for me. May everything you have told me come to pass." And the angel left her.*

Mary did not question the Angel of the Lord, she just received the prophetic instructions that were to come. I must say, I really admire that about Mary that she was able to receive the message without any doubts or fears. Even if she thought about the how, that's now a sign of doubt or fear, but a sign of curiosity about God's plan for her life.

Obedience is shown to God from the moment you hear his instructions for your life. What has God told you to do recently? Have you done it? If you have, great job. If you have not, why are you hesitating? Do you have a tendency to procrastinate? Being aware of what's hindering you is very important to know, so you can take it to God in prayer. Father God knows you, he's been waiting on you for quite some time now, please don't make him wait any longer. God wants us to come to him with those things that are hard for us to handle, he wants to transform us and make us better. We just have to partner with Father God in the process.

It's okay to ask God for clarification on his instructions. Sometimes he gives us prophetic instructions and messages that will come to pass at a much later date. When Father God gives you instructions it is okay to ask:

Is this something I start right away?

How do I prepare for this task?

What do you want me to do right now in this moment?

How exactly do you want me to complete this task?

You notice the questions never doubt God's instructions, but they help to gain better clarity on what is expected on carrying out the task.

Learning to obey God immediately helps to ward off procrastination, doubt and fear. When God can count on you to get the job done without hesitation, trust me he can use you for even bigger and greater assignments. Sometimes we want that great big assignment, but let's face it will take preparation. It is very rare for someone to start out on the mountaintop, they usually had to work hard and continue to work hard to get to the top. Well, the same can be said for growing and maturing in Christ Jesus. It takes prayer, time, money, energy and effort to become more spiritually mature. Take for example someone is told by God that they are a Pastor. It's important to remember that God sees us as we already are, even if we are not at that level yet. If the person jumps up gets business cards with the title Pastor and their name, most likely they have moved to quickly. When God said they were a Pastor, a more humble approach of receiving that message is:

Father God how do I prepare to be a Pastor with a spirit of excellence?

When will the door open for me to be an actual Pastor?

What type of Pastor are you calling me to be?

So, let's back track a bit in this example, let's say that God had told the same person a few years ago it's time to go to Bible College. However, the person has procrastinated and did not see the reason at the time to go to Bible College. When God tells us to do something it's better to obey, than to think that we know more than he does. Now look at the situation this way, the person would have been in a much better position to be a Pastor if they would have obeyed God many years ago and went to Bible College.

Let's be real we are living in the last of the last and evil days. It will take adequate training and preparation to fulfill the call of God on our lives. Bible College instructs on the scriptures, ministry and especially Pastoral ministry and the equipping is even better because of recent events too. So, if you find yourself reading this book it's not a coincidence. Whenever God gives you instructions especially when they are RIGHT NOW instructions, moving on them immediately is key.

If God has told you to go to Bible College here are some questions to ask him:

What Bible College should I attend?

How soon should I enroll?

What type of Biblical degree should I obtain?

What areas should I really focus on within my courses and degree?

Let me encourage you not to delay any longer, do what God has told you to do, go to Bible College. A good place to start is to do a Google search on local Bible Colleges and ask for recommendations from people who have already gone to Bible College.

Remember we talked about living a Godly example before God and others. When people see you obeying God immediately and without making excuses, that will help some to be motivated to do the same. I must say of the people that I have really admired in the Kingdom of God, they obeyed God and did what he told them to do WITHOUT HESITATION! I was amazed at how some were told to leave their job, restaurants, etc. and go into full time ministry; and they left lucrative positions, businesses and did what God told them to do! There will come a time where the rubber will meet the road, walking by faith and not by sight requires obedience. When God gives those more challenging instructions will you obey God without hesitation?

Obedience is faith and faith is obedience. It is hard to show God our faith without obedience. The scripture let us know it is impossible to please God without faith. Hebrews 11:6 *But without faith it is impossible to please him: for he that cometh to God must believe that he is, and that he is a rewarder of them that diligently seek him.* Abraham's faith was credited to him as righteousness. Genesis 15:6 KJV *And he believed in the LORD; and he counted it to him for righteousness.* When God told Abraham to go to a foreign land that he did not know, he had reasons to question God and not to obey. Yet Abraham trusted God, obeyed and went to the foreign land. To me it's no wonder that Abraham would end up with the name that meant "Father of many nations."

Genesis 17:4-6 KJV *As for me, behold, my covenant is with thee, and thou shalt be a father of many nations. Neither shall thy name any more be called Abram, but thy name shall be Abraham; for a father of many nations have I made thee. And I will make thee exceeding fruitful, and I will make nations of thee, and kings shall come out of thee.*

Those who obey God without hesitation have some of the most powerful praise reports, testimonies and greater works than those who don't. A word of encouragement here, you too can be fully utilized for God's glory through your obedience to him. When God speaks, get the clarification, and carry out his instructions without doubt, fear or hesitation.

Heavenly Father thank you for stressing the importance of obeying you immediately. Would you help me to be more like Mary and say I am the Lord's servant and may God's words be fulfilled in my life? Lord God may I be ready to receive your instructions wholeheartedly and seek your guidance to carry the plans out with a spirit of excellence. Father God, I desire to do the greater works that Jesus said I would do, please help me to complete each assignment efficiently and effectively as possible. Father God I want to please you with my faith, so I thank you in advance for blessing me with an increase in SUPERNATURAL OBEDIENCE. In Jesus Mighty Name Amen and Amen.

Chapter 5 Summary

When Is Obedience Shown to God?

- **IMMEDIATELY**

- **When you hear God's instructions receive them with gladness.**

- **Be determined in your heart to obey God without fail.**

- **It's okay to seek God for clarification, but still start where you can and continue until you finish the assignment.**

- **Those who obey God without hesitation have powerful praise reports, testimonies and greater works to show to the world!**

Chapter 6
Where Is Obedience Shown to God?

Where is obedience shown to God? That's a really good question. So, let's look at it this way, wherever you are remember to obey God right then and there. You could be at home, school, work, church, grocery store, park, vacation, hospital, nursing home, concert, etc. if God gives you specific instructions that's where you obey God, in those very places at that very moment.

As you read God's word you learn more about God's order and structure. As you learn those Biblical principles, that is the time to start putting them into practice. Since God is a God of order, it's important that we know that obedience first and foremost starts at home. Unfortunately some tend to think that the schools, after school clubs, are supposed to teach our children obedience. They are to help reinforce what they should already be learning at home.

God is the creator of family. It's time to get back to basics and our homes must be a place where obedience is demonstrated day in and day out. When obedience is not shown at home, a sincere prayer of repentance needs to go forth and show the children how even adults miss the mark and have to get back on track with Father God. Families should be striving to live an obedient life before God and others. Our children will stick with God and his ways if we as parents and adults show them the loving and obedient way to follow God.

If you work on a job, especially where there are unbelievers that is a real opportunity to shine brightly for Father God. When others aren't following the supervisor's instructions, as a Believer of God you should. We have to make the most of every opportunity to win souls for Jesus Christ. People notice that something is different about you any way so, let your obedience to God shine forth like the noon day. When they see you work with a spirit of excellence and refuse to join in with the gossiping and complaining, your co-workers will notice.

Be advised you can and most likely will come under fire for your obedience, but know that comes with the territory. We can't afford to wear our feelings on our sleeves anymore; we are in a spiritual warfare battle like never before. Therefore, we must do all that we can, while we can and continue to think with the end in mine. When they see you take time for prayer and Bible reading at lunch, trust me you will stand out. Plus people are looking for the real and living God.

May I encourage you they can find him in you but you must be willing to obey God, and do things his way.

Another place to show obedience is in the House of God or House of Prayer. As society loses touch with solid morals, values, decency and respect, that is why it is of utmost importance to show God the reverence he is due and respect the church too. Since God is a God of order it just makes sense to truly obey God in his house. Certain conversations, thoughts, attitudes and hidden agendas should not take place in God's House of Prayer. As Believers we should be making every effort to glorify Father God with our obedience to him, and especially in his house.

Even when we think no one is watching obedience to God is key. We want to make sure that God can count on us even when people are not looking or not around. A true Believer knows there is no escaping Father God, he sees and knows everything we do. So, when we get it deep in our hearts that obedience is required it will make a world of difference in the choices and decisions that we make.

Embracing prayer is a solid method of increasing our obedience to Father God. As we live our everyday lives it can be easy to lose sight of the fact that God is with us everywhere we go. Even when we think we can escape him, it's just not possible. Prayer will help us to stay on track and avoid the majority of the enemies pitfalls and traps for our lives. When God sees you earnestly and fervently seeking him in prayer to be more obedient to him, trust me Father God will take notice and that prayer will be answered. As time is winding down it is time to be more serious about our relationship with Father God, and do our best to show him obedience wherever we go.

Even Jesus had to accept the will of God for his life in the Garden of Gethsemane. As I read that text the anguish of Jesus just comes to life all the more for me. Jesus was often known to withdraw to secluded places like the Garden of Gethsemane to pray by himself with God the Father. Jesus and God were one, and even Jesus had to surrender his will right there in the garden! How much more will we have to obey Father God wherever we are? Read The Passion Translation scriptures below as reminder of Jesus's sacrifice and ultimate surrender of his own will, and obeyed Father God even until death on the cross.

Matthew 26:36-46 TPT *Then Jesus led his disciples to an orchard called "The Oil Press." He told them, "Sit here while I go and pray nearby." He took Peter, Jacob, and John with him. However, an intense feeling of great sorrow plunged his soul into agony. And he said to them, "My heart is overwhelmed and crushed with grief. It feels as though I'm dying. Stay here and* keep watch with me." Then he walked a short distance away, and overcome with grief, he threw himself facedown on the ground and prayed, "My Father, if there is any way you can deliver me from this suffering, please take it from me. **Yet what I want is not important, for I only desire to fulfill your plan for me."** Then an angel from heaven appeared to strengthen him. Later, he came back to his three disciples and found them all sound asleep. He awakened Peter and said to him, "Could you not stay awake with me for even one hour? Keep alert and pray that you'll be spared from this time of testing. Your spirit is eager enough, but your humanity is weak." Then he left them for a second time to pray in solitude. He said to God, **"My Father, if there is not a way that you can deliver me from this suffering, then your will must be done."** He came back to the disciples and found them sound asleep, for they couldn't keep their eyes open. So he left them and went away to pray the same prayer for the third time. When he returned again to his disciples, he awoke them, saying, "Are you still sleeping? Don't you know the hour has come for the Son of Man to be handed over to the authority of sinful men? Get up and let's go, for the betrayer has arrived.

Heavenly Father thank you for revealing to me the importance of obedience everywhere. Since I know you always see everything, I pray that you will always encourage and strengthen me to obey your word, ways, laws, commandments and specific instructions for my life. I desire to be the soul winner that you are calling me to be in this late hour, and I thank you for blessing me with the spiritual maturity to think with the end in mind. As I seek you for a SUPERNATURAL INCREASE IN OBEDIENCE I have no doubt that you will hear and answer my prayer. Father God thank you for the loving reminder to set my home in order by living and teaching obedience to my family on daily basis. Lord God, thank you that I will be humble to admit my wrongs, repent and get back on track with you and your perfected will for my life. In Jesus Mighty Name Amen and Amen.

Chapter 6 Summary

Where Is Obedience Shown to God?

- **EVERYWHERE**

- **It starts at home, living and teaching obedience before the family on a daily basis.**

- **Especially at work, win the unsaved for the Lord.**

  o **Remember Believers work unto the Lord, not mere man.**
  o **Believers should stand out at work for doing what is lawfully and reasonably asked of them.**
  o **Refuse to join in with the gossiping and complaining**

- **In the HOUSE OF GOD or HOUSE OF PRAYER, Father God is due the utmost respect, especially in his house.**
  o **Avoid certain conversations, gossiping, attitudes and hidden agendas**

- **Remember God sees everything you do, there is no escaping him.**

- **Obey God whether people are watching or not, because God is always watching.**

Chapter 7

Summary & Salvation Prayer

Thank you for going on this journey to a better understanding that OBEDIENCE IS REQUIRED. We live in times that really require our obedience to Father God. Remember that obedience is life and disobedience is death. If ever there were a time to be seeking the face of God the Father, now is that time. Be sure you know the GREAT SHEPHERD'S voice so you can obey when he speaks directly to you. We have to be so in tuned with the GREAT SHEPHERD'S voice that we refuse to follow any strange voices.

As time is winding down, entirely too much is at stake to walk in persistent disobedience, which truly is a form of rebellion. As we walk this faith walk, we should be desiring to be more obedient each and every day of our lives. There are so many blessings and benefits to living an obedient lifestyle before Father God and others. The exact opposite is true as well, there are so many consequences and punishments for living a disobedient lifestyle before Father God and others. Now, is the time to decide to live fully for God Almighty, that you will give him your very best and nothing less. When the rubber meets the road, will you be found in the group that decided I will obey God until the day that I die?

Simply put it just costs a Believer in Christ too much not to obey God. The world needs to see God's children doing their best to uplift him and obey his laws, commandments and instructions. Our children need to see adults that have a true reverence for Father God, through an obedient and loving lifestyle. Can God count on you to be in that faithful, but tried and true group that lives and dies for Almighty God. That you can stand on Joshua 24:15 without fail:

And if it seem evil unto you to serve the L*ord,* *choose you this day whom ye will serve; whether the gods which your fathers served that were on the other side of the flood, or the gods of the Amorites, in whose land ye dwell: but as for me and my house, we will serve the* L*ord.*

Knowing totally and fully you cannot serve Father God without obeying him.

Below are some obedience scriptures that will be useful to pray, meditate, memorize and live as one walks on this journey.

Obedience Scriptures

Exodus 19:5 KJV *Now therefore, if ye will obey my voice indeed, and keep my covenant, then ye shall be a peculiar treasure unto me above all people: for all the earth is mine:*

2 Corinthians 10:5 TPT *We can demolish every deceptive fantasy that opposes God and break through every arrogant attitude that is raised up in defiance of the true knowledge of God. We capture, like prisoners of war, every thought and insist that it bow in obedience to the Anointed One.*

Ephesians 6:1-3 KJV *Children, obey your parents in the Lord: for this is right. Honour thy father and mother; which is the first commandment with promise; That it may be well with thee, and thou mayest live long on the earth.*

2 John 1:6 TPT *This love means living in obedience to whatever God commands us. For to walk in love toward one another is the unifying commandment we've heard from the beginning.*

Joshua 5:6 NLT *The Israelites had traveled in the wilderness for forty years until all the men who were old enough to fight in battle when they left Egypt had died. For they had disobeyed the Lord, and the Lord vowed he would not let them enter the land he had sworn to give us—a land flowing with milk and honey.*

Luke 11:28 TPT *"Yes," said Jesus, "but God will bless all who listen to the word of God and carefully obey everything they hear."*

Romans 5:19 TPT *One man's disobedience opened the door for all humanity to become sinners. So also one man's obedience opened the door for many to be made perfectly right with God and acceptable to him.*

James 1:25 AMP *But he who looks carefully into the perfect law, the law of liberty, and faithfully abides by it, not having become a [careless] listener who forgets but an active doer [who obeys], he will be blessed and favored by God in what he does [in his life of obedience].*

1 Peter 1:14 NLT *So you must live as God's obedient children. Don't slip back into your old ways of living to*

satisfy your own desires. You didn't know any better then.

Philippians 2:8 KJV *And being found in fashion as a man, he humbled himself, and became obedient unto death, even the death of the cross.*

John 14:23 TPT *Jesus replied, "Loving me empowers you to obey my word. And my Father will love you so deeply that we will come to you and make you our dwelling place.*

1 Kings 2:3 TLB *Obey the laws of God and follow all his ways; keep each of his commands written in the law of Moses so that you will prosper in everything you do, wherever you turn.*

Joshua 1:8 NLT *Study this Book of Instruction continually. Meditate on it day and night so you will be sure to obey everything written in it. Only then will you prosper and succeed in all you do.*

Psalm 128:1 TPT *How joyous are those who love the Lord and bow low before God, ready to obey him!*

Psalm 128:1 TLB Blessings on all who reverence and trust the Lord—on all who obey him!

We want to make the most of every opportunity to win souls for Jesus Christ. The truth is eternity is closer for some than others. We are not just living for this life, but we are surely living for the life to come. Let me encourage you do not delay in saying this Salvation Prayer. Please repeat this prayer from a sincere heart.

Dear Lord Jesus, I know that I am a sinner, and I ask you for your forgiveness. I believe you died for my sins and rose from the dead. I turn from my sins, and invite You to come into my heart and life. I ask for the Holy Spirit to dwell in me, to guide me, and to teach me all things. I choose to trust and follow You as the Son of God and LORD and Savior in Jesus name Amen and Amen.

If you repeated that prayer with a true sincerity you JUST GOT SAVED!!! We encourage you to read your Bible on a daily basis. Here are your next steps:

1) **Download the free Bible App https://www.youversion.com/the-bible-app/.**
2) **Get a paper Parallel Study Bible that has King James Version(KJV) and another version of your choice that helps you to understand the scriptures better.**
3) **Read the Bible every day.**
4) **Ask God the Father to lead you to a church home where the Bible is taught and preached in a way that you can understand it and live it out daily.**

Lastly if you repeated the Salvation Prayer and got saved please email us at itsprayingtime2020@gmail.com, we would like to pray for you and encourage you along your spiritual journey. You can also email us your prayer requests and we would be glad to stand in the gap for you.

Author's Biography

Dr. Kimberly K. Clayton is determined to obey God, because she understands obedience is required. She is currently working on another biblical project with goals to represent Jesus Christ to the fullest, win as many souls for Jesus Christ as possible, recruit and train additional godly intercessors, and to continue to pray and intercede as God has called her to do. She lives with her daughter, Elise, who is her pride and joy!

She is the founder and leader of "It's Praying Time," a ministry where prayer intercession and training takes place on a weekly basis. Dr. Kimberly believes in the power of prayer and intercession and is determined to help others grow in this calling through the prayer line, Facebook Live and YouTube. You are welcome to become a subscriber to our "It's Praying Time" You Tube Channel. "It's Praying Time" is focused on reaching as many people as possible for Jesus Christ through various means and platforms.

Dr. Kimberly Clayton is also an ordained and licensed minister through the "School of the Prophet" which is led by their fearless leader, Prophetess Renee Gordon. One of Kimberly's most prized moments is when she and her young daughter, Elise, had their second baptism together through the "School of the Prophet". She also treasures being able to serve on other prayer lines when needed.